irresistible
biscuits
cookies & shortbread

Everyone loves freshly baked biscuits. Their rich, buttery taste and
crisp texture are perfect to partner mid-morning tea or coffee.
In *Irresistible Biscuits, Cookies & Shortbread* we bring you
a selection of old-time favourites and delicious new ideas.
Our step-by-step illustrations will help you along the way,
so the biscuit barrel need never be empty again.

PERIPLUS

SWEET BISCUITS

Everyone loves the buttery taste and brittle texture of homemade biscuits – they make great snacks any time of day. They are also welcome gifts and useful contributions to picnics, parties and get-togethers.

The word 'biscuit' comes from the French *bis cuit* which means 'twice cooked' possibly originating from the fact that the 'biscuits' were cooked twice to keep fresh and crisp for long periods, especially for travellers undertaking long voyages at sea.

When making biscuits or any of the other goodies in this book, it helps to measure accurately. Our recipes have been tested using standard metric measuring cups and spoons. These, and graduated glass or plastic jugs (for measuring liquids), are available from cookware shops, department stores and major grocers. For dry ingredients, spoon into measuring cups or spoons, then level with a spatula.

 Always use the graduated jug for liquid ingredients.

Correct storage of biscuits is also important; note the storage techniques outlined in cookies.

Basic Biscuit Dough

Preparation time:
  25 minutes
Cooking time:
  15 minutes
Makes about 40

125 g butter
½ cup sugar
3 tablespoons milk
¼ teaspoon imitation
  vanilla essence
1½ cups self-raising
  flour, sifted
½ cup custard
  powder

1 Beat butter and sugar in a bowl with an electric beater until light and fluffy. Add milk and vanilla essence; beat well.
2 Fold in sifted flour and custard powder until well combined.
3 Place some of the mixture into a biscuit press with desired nozzle attached (see Note). Form biscuits by pressing onto greased baking trays.
4 Bake at 200°C for 12-15 minutes, or until golden brown. Cool on trays for 2-3 minutes.

Transfer to a wire rack to cool completely. Store in an airtight container.

Note: Fill biscuit press according to the manufacturer's instructions. Alternatively, roll the mixture into walnut-sized balls. Place on lightly greased baking trays. Flatten the top of each biscuit with a floured fork, then bake as directed.

Variations:
◆ Cinnamon: Replace one tablespoon flour with one of cocoa. Add one teaspoon ground cinnamon when adding the flour.
◆ Coconut: Add ½ cup coconut in Step 2.
◆ Coffee: Dissolve two teaspoons of coffee powder in three teaspoons hot water. Reduce milk by three teaspoons. Add coffee mixture with milk.
◆ Lemon: Add grated rind of ½ lemon, one teaspoon of lemon juice and a few drops of yellow food colouring in Step 1.
◆ Walnut: Using the basic dough, roll into walnut-sized balls. Place on lightly greased baking trays. Flatten with a floured fork and top with a walnut half to decorate.

A selection of biscuits including Walnut, Cinnamon, Coffee, Lemon, Coconut & Plain

Melting Moments

Preparation time:
  15 minutes
Cooking time:
  15 minutes
Makes about 35

½ cup cornflour
1½ cups self-raising
  flour
⅓ cup icing sugar, sifted
1 egg
½ teaspoon imitation
  vanilla essence
155 g butter, melted

1 Sift together flour
and cornflour. Put half
in a bowl and mix in
sifted icing sugar, egg
and vanilla. Stir in
melted butter and beat
for 2-3 minutes. Stir in
remaining sifted flour
and mix to a firm
dough.
2 Roll small portions
into balls and place on
greased baking trays,
allow room for
spreading. Lightly
flatten the top of each
biscuit with a fork.
Bake at 180°C for 15
minutes, or until lightly
browned. Cool on trays
for 2-3 minutes.
Transfer to a wire rack.
Cool completely. Store
in an airtight container.

Ginger Biscuits

Preparation time:
  3 0 minutes
Cooking time:
  15 minutes
Makes about 48

125 g butter
¼ cup treacle
2 cups plain flour
2 teaspoons ground
  ginger
1 teaspoon bicarbonate
  of soda
⅓ cup sugar
1 egg
chopped glacé ginger
125g chocolate, melted

1 In a small pan, stir
together butter and
treacle until melted.
2 Sift together flour,
ginger and soda in a
mixing bowl. Stir in
sugar. Add syrup
mixture and egg. Beat
until combined.
3 Roll heaped
teaspoonfuls of dough
into small balls.
Arrange on greased
baking trays. Flatten
slightly with a fork.
Press a small piece of
ginger into the centre of
each biscuit.
4 Bake at 180°C for
12-15 minutes until
golden. Cool slightly on
tray. Remove to a wire
rack, cool completely.
Drizzle melted
chocolate over biscuits.
Let stand until firm.

Peanutty Bars

Preparation time:
  20 minutes
Cooking time:
  15 minutes
Makes about 36

Clockwise from top: Melting Moments, Peanutty Bars & Mexican Sand Biscuits

1 cup crunchy peanut butter
¾ cup sugar
1 egg
1 teaspoon imitation vanilla essence
¼ cup milk
¼ cup plain flour
¼ cup chopped unsalted peanuts

1 Place peanut butter, sugar, egg, vanilla, milk and flour in bowl of a food processor and combine until mixture holds together. Stir in peanuts.
2 Press mixture into a greased 30 x 23 cm shallow oblong baking tray. Use a sharp knife to mark mixture into 4 cm long fingers. Bake at 160°C for 15 minutes or until lightly browned. Carefully remove biscuits from baking tray. Cool on wire racks. Store in an airtight container.

5

For Anzacs: combine oats, flour, sugar and coconut in a large bowl.

Add combined melted butter, golden syrup, water and soda to flour mixture.

Anzacs

Preparation time:
  20 minutes
Cooking time:
  20 minutes
Makes about 50

1 *cup rolled oats*
1 *cup plain flour, sifted*
1 *cup sugar*
3/4 *cup desiccated*
  coconut
150 *g butter*
2 *tablespoons golden*
  syrup
2 *tablespoons boiling*
  water
1 1/2 *teaspoons*
  bicarbonate of soda

1 Combine oats, sifted flour, sugar and coconut in a large bowl. Melt butter and golden syrup together in a small pan.
2 Mix boiling water and soda together. Blend into butter mixture. Pour over dry ingredients; mix well.
3 Place spoonfuls of mixture onto greased baking trays, allow room for spreading.
4 Bake at 150°C for 15-20 minutes, or until golden. Loosen while warm. Cool on trays Transfer to a wire rack Cool completely. Store in an airtight container.

Mexican Sand Biscuits

Preparation time:
  25 minutes
Cooking time:
  8 minutes
Makes about 20

125 *g butter*
1/3 *cup icing sugar, sifted*
1 *egg yolk*
1 *tablespoon brandy*
1/2 *teaspoon ground*
  cinnamon

2 *cups plain flour, sifted*
extra sifted icing sugar,
  for dusting

1 Beat butter and icing sugar in a large bowl with an electric mixer until light and fluffy. Add egg yolk, brandy and cinnamon; mix well. Fold in sifted flour and stir until a soft dough is formed.
2 Roll dough into oval shapes about 5 cm long and 2 cm thick and bend into crescents. Place on a greased baking tray, allow room for spreading.
3 Bake at 150°C for 8 minutes until biscuits are firm and pale golden (do not allow to brown). Remove to a wire rack to cool slightly.
4 Roll warm biscuits in extra icing sugar to coat; cool completely. Store in an airtight container. Lightly dust again with icing sugar just before serving.

Place spoonfuls of mixture onto greased baking trays. Allow room for spreading.

Transfer biscuits to a wire rack to cool completely.

Chocolate Wheats

Preparation time:
40 minutes
Cooking time:
12 minutes
Makes about 30

1¼ *cups wholemeal
plain flour, sifted*
⅔ *cup white self-raising
flour, sifted*
1 *teaspoon baking
powder*
1 *tablespoon sugar*
120 *g butter*
a little milk, for mixing
125 *g dark chocolate,
melted*

1 In a food processor or
large bowl, mix together
sifted flour, baking
powder, sugar and butter
until mixture resembles
coarse breadcrumbs.
2 Gradually add just
enough milk to give a
firm, dry dough that can
be shaped into a ball.
3 On a lightly floured
surface, knead dough
briefly, then roll out to
3 mm thick. Cut into
rounds with a fluted
medium scone cutter. Use
a smaller cutter to cut
out centre of rounds.
Place on greased and
floured baking trays;
pierce all over with a
fork, allow room for
spreading.
4 Bake at 190°C for
10-12 minutes, or until
lightly browned. Cool on
tray for 2-3 minutes.
Transfer to a wire rack
to cool completely.
5 Drizzle melted
chocolate over biscuits.
Let stand until firm.
Store in an airtight
container.

Cut Out Biscuits

Preparation time:
35 minutes + 3 hours
chilling
Cooking time:
7 minutes
Makes about 60

125 *g butter*
½ *cup caster sugar*
1 *egg*
½ *cup treacle*
1½ *teaspoons vinegar*
3 *cups plain flour*
2 *teaspoons
bicarbonate of soda*
1½ *teaspoons ground
ginger*
½ *teaspoon ground
cinnamon*
½ *teaspoon ground
cloves*

Lemon icing
1 *egg white*
½ *teaspoon lemon juice*
1¼ *cups icing sugar,
sifted*
yellow food colouring

1 Beat butter, sugar and
egg in a mixing bowl
with an electric mixer
until light and fluffy.
Add treacle and vinegar;
mix well.
2 Sift together flour and
remaining ingredients;
gradually stir into egg
mixture until combined.
3 Shape dough into two
equal balls; wrap and
chill for three hours.
4 On a lightly floured
surface, roll out dough,
half at a time, to 3 mm
thickness. Cut into
desired shapes using a
sharp knife or cut-outs.
5 Place 5 cm apart on
ungreased baking trays.
Bake at 190°C for 5-7
minutes. Cool on wire
racks.
6 To make lemon icing:
beat egg white until
foamy. Add lemon juice
and icing sugar and
beat until thick and
creamy. Tint the mixture
lemon using food
colours. Pipe onto
biscuits through a fine
pointed cone, shaped
from greaseproof or
baking paper.

> ## Hint
> When shaping dough into balls or crescents, use
> cool hands dusted with flour. Don't overwork it,
> as the dough may toughen and crack when
> baked. If dough is very sticky, roll out with a
> rolling pin between two sheets of greaseproof
> paper or plastic film.

Left: Chocolate Wheats.
Right: Cut Out Biscuits.

Liqueur Biscuits

Preparation time:
  45 minutes
Cooking time:
  7 minutes
Makes about 20

250 g butter
1/2 cup icing sugar, sifted
1/2 teaspoon imitation
  rum essence
2 cups plain flour, sifted
1/4 teaspoon
  baking powder

Filling
1 cup thickened cream
1 tablespoon icing sugar
2 teaspoons rum

1 Cream butter, icing sugar and rum until light and fluffy. Sift together flour and baking powder, and gradually stir into creamed mixture until ingredients are well mixed.
2 Place dough in a pastry bag fitted with a large star tube. Press out to form 4 cm lengths on prepared trays. If dough does not press smoothly, stir in two teaspoons softened butter. Bake for 5-7 minutes until edges start to brown. Cool for five minutes on trays before turning out onto wire racks to cool further.
3 To prepare filling: beat cream, icing sugar and rum together until thick. Join two fingers together with filling. Repeat with remaining biscuits.

Fruity Oat Biscuits

Preparation time:
  15 minutes
Cooking time:
  15 minutes
Makes about 50

125 g butter
3/4 cup caster sugar
1 egg
1 cup finely grated
  carrot
1/4 cup finely chopped
  pecans
1/2 cup currants
1 cup self-raising flour
1/4 cup plain flour
1 teaspoon ground
  cinnamon
1/4 teaspoon ground
  cloves
3/4 cup quick cooking
  oats
1/4-1/2 cup buttermilk

1 Preheat oven to 190°C and grease oven trays.
2 Cream butter, add sugar and egg and beat well. Stir in carrot, pecans, currants and three-quarters of sifted dry ingredients. Add oats, remaining sifted dry ingredients and sufficient buttermilk to make a firm dough.
3 Place slightly heaped teaspoonfuls of mixture at intervals

For Liqueur Biscuits stir flour and baking powder into creamed mixture.

Using a piping bag fitted with a star tube, pipe mixture to 4 cm lengths.

Join two fingers together with filling. Repeat with remaining biscuits.

Top: Fruity Oat Biscuits
Bottom: Liqueur Biscuits

on prepared trays, press down tops with a fork and bake 12-15 minutes or until golden brown.

4 Cool on trays 10 minutes before removing to a cake rack.

Cool completely. These biscuits may be iced with a lemon glacé icing, if desired. Store in an airtight container for up to 5 days.

HINT
Limp or stale biscuits can sometimes be revived by heating in the oven for 5 minutes.

Crispy Oatmeal Biscuits

Crispy Oatmeal Biscuits

Preparation time:
  35 minutes
Cooking time:
  20 minutes
Makes about 24

1 cup wholemeal plain
  flour
1 teaspoon baking
  powder
1 teaspoon mixed spice
1 egg
½ cup skim milk
1 teaspoon liquid
  artificial sweetener
80 g butter
*½ teaspoon imitation
  vanilla essence*
*3 breakfast cereal
  biscuits, crushed*
1 cup rolled oats

1 Sift together flour, baking powder and spice; add husks from sifter to bowl and set aside.
2 Beat egg, milk, sweetener and vanilla essence.
3 In another bowl, beat butter with one tablespoon of flour mixture until creamy. Add remaining dry ingredients alternately with egg mixture, stirring until blended.
4 Stir in breakfast cereal biscuits and oats, mixing to a stiff dough. Knead gently. On a floured surface, roll out dough to 5 mm thickness.
5 Cut into 24 rounds with a scone cutter. Place on a greased baking tray. Allow room for spreading. Bake in a moderately hot oven (190°C) for 15-20 minutes or until crisp and golden. Cool completely on the tray. Store in an airtight container.

Chocolate Wafers

Note: A few finely chopped apricots or other dried fruit can be pressed on to biscuits to decorate before baking, if desired.

Chocolate Wafers

Preparation time:
  40 minutes
Cooking time:
  12 minutes
Makes about 12

1/4 cup brown sugar
1/4 cup sugar
3 egg whites

2 tablespoons plain
  flour, sifted
1 tablespoon cocoa
2 tablespoons thickened
  cream
60 g butter, melted
1/2 cup slivered almonds

1 Beat sugars and egg whites in a small bowl with an electric mixer until frothy. Beat in sifted flour and cocoa, then cream and butter. Leave mixture to stand for 10 minutes.

2 Spoon about two teaspoonfuls of mixture onto each end of paper-lined baking sheets. Allow room for spreading. Spread out mixture to form 12 cm circles. Arrange almond slivers on top.
3 Bake at 160°C for 10-12 minutes, or until edges begin to darken. Cool on tray for 2-3 minutes. Transfer to a wire rack. Store in an airtight container.

HINT
Biscuits make excellent presents, wrapped in a clean, new tea-towel or placed in a pretty tin.

Burnt Butter Biscuits

Preparation time:
  30 minutes
Cooking time:
  15 minutes
Makes about 20

125 g butter
1/2 cup caster sugar
1 teaspoon imitation
  vanilla essence
1 egg
1 1/4 cups self-raising
  flour, sifted
blanched almonds

1 Melt butter in a pan over low heat. When butter turns light brown, remove and cool slightly.
2 Beat in sugar. Add vanilla essence and egg; mix until smooth. Fold in sifted flour and combine well.
3 Roll dough into small balls. Place on greased baking trays, allow room for spreading. Press an almond in the centre of each ball.
4 Bake at 180°C for 15 minutes, or until golden. Cool on trays for 2-3 minutes. Transfer to a wire rack to cool completely. Store in an airtight container.

Monte Carlos

Preparation time:
  35 minutes + cooling time
Cooking time:
  12 minutes
Makes about 15

125 g butter
1/2 cup sugar
1 egg
1 teaspoon imitation
  vanilla essence
2 cups self-raising flour,
  sifted
3/4 cup plain flour, sifted
raspberry jam

Filling
60 g butter
3/4 cup icing sugar, sifted
1 teaspoon imitation
  vanilla essence
2 teaspoons milk

1 Beat butter and sugar in a small bowl with an electric mixer until it is creamy. Add egg and beat well. Beat in vanilla. Fold in sifted flours and mix well.
2 Roll teaspoonfuls of mixture into balls. Place on greased baking trays, allow room for spreading. Lightly flatten the top of each biscuit with a fork. Bake at 180°C for 10-12 minutes, or until golden. Cool on trays for 2-3 minutes. Transfer to a wire rack to cool completely. When cold, sandwich biscuits together with filling.
3 To make filling: beat butter and icing sugar in a small bowl until creamy. Add vanilla and milk, beating well. Spread over half the biscuits and top with remaining biscuits. Store in an airtight container.

> **HINT**
> Always allow biscuits to cool completely before storing in airtight containers.

Fruity Florentines

Preparation time:
  35 minutes
Cooking time:
  20 minutes
Makes about 15

> **HINT**
> Mix well but lightly. You can use a wooden spoon or an electric mixer to cream butter and sugar mixtures and to beat in eggs or essence. Stir in dry ingredients with the spoon just until combined as mixers tend to overwork the dough.

Clockwise from top left: Orange Biscuits, Anzacs, Monte Carlos, Fruity Florentines & Burnt Butter Biscuits

80 g butter
1/2 cup caster sugar
1/3 cup milk
1/2 cup plain flour, sifted
1/4 cup sultanas
1/4 cup glacé cherries, roughly chopped
1/4 cup mixed peel
50 g flaked almonds
150 g dark chocolate, chopped

1 Combine butter, sugar and milk in a pan and heat gently until butter melts, then bring to the boil. Remove from heat and cool for 3 minutes. Add sifted flour and stir until smooth, then add sultanas, mixed peel, cherries and almonds.
2 Drop tablespoons of mixture on greased baking trays, allow room for spreading. Bake at 180°C for 15-20 minutes, or until golden brown. Cool on trays for 2-3 minutes.

Transfer to a wire rack to cool completely.
3 Melt chocolate in a bowl over hot water. Spread evenly over flat side of biscuits and mark lines in it with a fork. Leave until chocolate hardens before serving. Store in an airtight container.

HINT
When creaming butter and sugar mixtures do not over cream, beat only until light and fluffy. Over beating will result in the mixture being too soft, causing the biscuits to spread too much during baking.

15

Orange Biscuits

Preparation time:
   35 minutes
Cooking time:
   15 minutes
Makes 12

125 g butter
¼ cup icing sugar
½ cup cornflour, sifted
½ cup plain flour, sifted

Filling
20 g butter
½ cup icing sugar
rind of 1 orange, finely
   grated
2 teaspoons orange juice

1 Beat butter with icing sugar in a bowl until creamy. Fold in sifted flours; combine thoroughly.
2 Drop teaspoonfuls of mixture onto greased baking trays. Lightly flatten the top of each biscuit with a fork. Bake at 180°C for 10-15 minutes, or until golden. Cool on tray for 2-3 minutes. Transfer to a wire rack to cool completely. When cold, sandwich biscuits together with orange filling.
3 To make filling: beat butter, icing sugar and orange rind in a small bowl with an electric mixer. Stir in orange juice. Spread over half the biscuits. Sandwich with remaining biscuits. Store in an airtight container.

HINT
In very humid conditions, store biscuits in containers in the refrigerator, for the best flavour and texture.

Peanut Biscuits

Preparation time:
   35 minutes
Cooking time:
   12 minutes
Makes about 30

125 g butter
½ cup crunchy peanut
   butter
½ cup brown sugar
2 tablespoons honey
1 egg
½ teaspoon imitation
   vanilla essence
1½ cups self-raising
   flour, sifted
1 cup unsalted peanuts

1 Beat butter and peanut butter in a small bowl with an electric mixer until creamy. Add sugar, honey, egg and vanilla; mix well.
2 Fold in sifted flour, stir in peanuts; mix well. Drop heaped tablespoonfuls of mixture onto greased baking trays, allow about 4 cm between mixture for spreading.
3 Bake at 180°C for 10-12 minutes, or until golden. Allow to cool on tray for 2-3 minutes. Cool completely on a wire rack. Store in an airtight container.

Easter Biscuits
These biscuits are traditionally served on Good Friday in Corsica, where they are known as *Fugazzi*. The originals are baked with pastis, a licorice-flavoured liqueur, but Pernod or ouzo will give the same flavoursome results.

Preparation time:
   25 minutes
Cooking time:
   20 minutes
Makes about 36

2 cups plain flour, sifted
½ cup sugar
⅓ cup vegetable oil
3 tablespoons white
   wine
2 tablespoons Pernod
   or milk
almond slivers

1 Combine sifted flour and sugar in a large mixing bowl. Make a well in centre of dry ingredients.
2 Combine oil, wine and Pernod; stir into

Top: Peanut Biscuits & Easter Biscuits

dry ingredients then knead mixture until smooth. Shape into a ball.
3 Roll out half the dough at a time on a lightly floured surface to 5 mm thick. Cut into rounds with a cutter. Press edges lightly with a fork or knife; pierce well all over with a fork.
4 Place on greased baking trays; place almond slivers on each biscuit. Bake at 180°C for 15-20 minutes, or until golden brown. Cool completely on wire racks.
Store in an airtight container.

Date and Walnut Biscuits

Preparation time:
  20 minutes
Cooking time:
  12 minutes
Makes about 50

180 g butter
1/2 cup caster sugar
1 egg
1 1/2 cups self-raising
  flour, sifted
1 teaspoon ground
  cinnamon
1/2 cup finely chopped
  dates
1/2 cup finely chopped
  walnuts
walnut halves

1 Beat butter and sugar in a small bowl with an electric mixer until light and fluffy. Add egg, beat until well combined.
2 Stir in sifted flour and cinnamon. Stir in dates and chopped walnuts; mix well.
3 Roll tablespoons of mixture into balls, place onto greased baking trays, allow room for spreading. Lightly flatten the top of each biscuit with a fork. Place a walnut half into the centre of each biscuit.
4 Bake at 190°C for about 10-12 minutes, or until golden brown. Cool on trays for 2-3 minutes. Transfer to a wire rack to cool completely. Store in an airtight container.

Coconut Almond Macaroons

Preparation time:
  15 minutes
Cooking time:
  12 minutes
Makes about 35

2 egg whites
1/2 cup icing sugar
1/2 cup shredded coconut
1/2 cup desiccated
  coconut
1/2 cup ground almonds
1/4 cup flaked almonds
1/4 cup choc bits

1 Beat egg whites until soft peaks form, add icing sugar gradually, beating well after each addition.
2 Stir in coconut, almonds and choc bits. Drop tablespoonfuls of mixture onto greased baking trays, allow room for spreading.
3 Bake at 180°C for about 10-12 minutes or until lightly golden. Cool on trays for 1-2 minutes. Transfer to wire rack to cool completely.

Left: Date and Walnut Biscuits   Right: Coconut Almond Macaroons

Mixed Spice Twists,
Vanilla Cherry Drops

Mixed Spice Twists

Preparation time:
  20 minutes
Cooking time:
  15 minutes
Makes about 24

125 g butter
1/2 cup brown sugar
1 egg
1 tablespoon golden
  syrup
1 1/2 teaspoons mixed
  spice
1 teaspoon ground
  ginger
2 1/4 cups self-raising
  flour
icing sugar

1 Beat butter and sugar until light and fluffy, add egg and golden syrup, beat until well combined.
2 Fold sifted spices and flour into creamed mixture. Roll level tablespoons of mixture into small oblongs.

Continue rolling into long rope shapes about 8 cm in length, fold in half and twist. Refrigerate mixture for 20 minutes.
3 Bake at 180°C for 12-15 minutes or until golden. Cool on trays for 2 minutes. Transfer to wire rack to cool completely. Dust with icing sugar to serve.

Vanilla Cherry Drops

Preparation time:
  20 minutes
Cooking time:
  15 minutes
Makes about 30

125 g butter
3/4 cup icing sugar

2 teaspoons imitation
  vanilla essence
3/4 cup plain flour
1/2 cup custard powder
about 15 red glacé
  cherries, halved
1/3 cup slivered almonds

1 Beat butter, icing sugar and vanilla until light and fluffy. Fold in the sifted flour and custard powder. Roll level tablespoons of the mixture into small rounds
2 Place on greased baking trays, allow room for spreading. Lightly flatten the top of each biscuit with two fingers, place a cherry half and two slivers of almonds into the centre of each biscuit.
3 Bake at 150°C for 12-15 minutes or until lightly golden. Cool on trays for 2-3 minutes. Transfer to a wire rack to cool completely. Store in an airtight container.

For Mixed Spice Twists: roll mixture into small oblong shapes.

Continue rolling into rope shapes about 8 cm in length, fold in half and twist.

21

SAVOURY BISCUITS

Savoury biscuits are a marvellous addition to the pantry. Delicious served plain, buttered or topped with cheese, pickled onions, gherkins or pâté, these biscuits are always popular with the family and useful when entertaining.

The dough is usually made of flour and butter and spiced up with celery salt, cayenne, seeds (sesame, poppy or caraway) and strongly flavoured cheeses like Parmesan or sharp Cheddar cheese. Many different types of flour can also be used for variety, e.g. plain, wholemeal, rye, cornmeal or oatmeal.

Baking and storage techniques are similar to those used with cookies and sweet biscuits.

Poppy Seed Crescents

Preparation time:
  25 minutes
Cooking time:
  10 minutes
Makes about 60

2 cups plain flour
1 teaspoon baking
  powder
125 g butter
1/2 cup grated Cheddar
  cheese
2 tablespoons French
  onion soup mix
1 egg, beaten
1/4 cup water or milk
extra beaten egg, for
  glazing
poppy seeds

1 Sift flour and baking powder into a mixing bowl. Add butter and rub in with fingertips. Stir in cheese, soup mix, egg and water. Mix to a dough.
2 Roll out dough on a floured surface to a thickness of 5 mm. Cut into crescents or other shapes. Place on a greased baking tray. Allow room for spreading. Brush with extra beaten egg and sprinkle with the poppy seeds.
3 Bake at 200°C for 10 minutes, or until golden brown. Cool on tray for 2-3 minutes. Transfer to a wire rack to cool completely. Store in an airtight container.

> ### HINT
> The recipes in this book use 55 g eggs unless otherwise specified.

Sesame Wafers

Preparation time:
  30 minutes + 1 hour
  chilling
Cooking time:
  10-12 minutes
Makes about 40

2 cups plain flour
2 teaspoons baking
  powder
1/4 teaspoon cayenne
1/2 teaspoon salt
125 g butter
1 cup grated Cheddar
  cheese
2 egg yolks
1-2 tablespoons lemon
  juice
1 egg white, lightly
  beaten
sesame seeds

1 Sift flour, baking powder, cayenne and salt into a bowl. Rub in butter with fingertips. Add the grated cheese and mix well.
2 Beat egg yolks with one tablespoon lemon juice. Mix into dry ingredients, adding extra lemon juice if necessary to make a firm dough.
3 Shape dough into a ball, cover with plastic film and chill for one hour. Turn out onto a floured surface and knead lightly.
4 Roll out thinly and cut into small rounds with a fluted cutter.

Poppy Seed Crescents & Sesame Wafers

Place on greased baking trays. Allow room for spreading. Brush with egg white and dust with sesame seeds.

5 Bake at 190°C for 10-12 minutes, or until golden. Loosen on the trays and cool for 2-3 minutes. Transfer to a wire rack to cool completely. Store in an airtight container.

> ### HINT
> Many biscuits freeze well both before and after baking.

Herbed Pretzels

Preparation time:
  25 minutes
Cooking time:
  15 minutes
Makes about 25

40 g butter, softened
1 tablespoon each
  chopped parsley,
  chives and rosemary
1 clove garlic, crushed
pepper to taste
2 sheets ready-rolled
  puff pastry, thawed
20 g extra butter, melted
2 tablespoons poppy
  seeds

1 Combine butter, herbs, garlic and pepper in a small bowl, and mix well.
2 Spread mixture

evenly over one sheet of pastry, coating completely. Top with remaining pastry. Press edges to seal. Brush top with melted butter. Sprinkle with poppy seeds.

3 Cut pastry into 2 cm wide strips. Twist each strip from both ends to make spirals. Place on an ungreased baking tray.

4 Bake at 230°C for 10-15 minutes, or until golden brown. Store in an airtight container. Serve warm or cold.

Savoury Bites

Preparation time:
  15 minutes
Cooking time:
  15 minutes
Makes about 40

1 cup coarsely grated,
  Cheddar cheese
125 g butter, chopped
1 cup rice flour
1 cup plain flour, sifted
1/4 teaspoon salt
1/2 teaspoon Tabasco
  sauce

1 Put cheese in a bowl with butter, rice flour, sifted flour, salt and Tabasco sauce. Combine to make a dough.
2 Roll dough into small balls. Place on greased baking trays.

Allow room for spreading. Bake at 180°C for 10-15 minutes, or until lightly browned.

3 Cool on trays for 2-3 minutes. Transfer to a wire rack to cool completely. Store in an airtight container.

Savoury Strips

Preparation time:
  25 minutes
Cooking time:
  20 minutes
Makes about 60

1/2 cup plain flour, sifted
1/2 cup self-raising
  flour, sifted
1/2 teaspoon salt
1/4 teaspoon paprika
1/4 teaspoon cayenne
11/2 cups grated,
  matured Cheddar
  cheese
1 egg
1/4 cup beer
extra beer, for brushing
coarse salt, for
  sprinkling

1 Combine sifted flours in a mixing bowl with salt, paprika, cayenne and cheese. Beat egg lightly in a small bowl and stir in beer. Pour over dry ingredients and mix to a firm dough.
2 Knead dough lightly on a floured surface. Roll out thinly and cut into 1 x 5cm wide

Top: Savoury Bites
Left: Herbed Pretzels
Right: Savoury Strips

strips. Place on an ungreased baking tray. Brush lightly with extra beer. Sprinkle with salt.

3 Bake at 180°C for 15-20 minutes, or until golden. Cool on trays for 2-3 minutes.

Transfer to a wire rack to cool completely. Store in an airtight container.

Back: Graham Crackers
Front: Caraway Twists

Graham Crackers

Here's the recipe for one of America's favourite savoury biscuits – top them with sweet or savoury spreads or enjoy them plain.

Preparation time:
  25 minutes + 30 minutes chilling
Cooking time:
  7 minutes
Makes about 60

2¹⁄₃ cups wholemeal plain flour
½ cup cornflour
½ teaspoon salt
¼ cup caster sugar
150 g butter
¾ cup cream

1 Sift flour, cornflour, salt and caster sugar into a bowl.
2 Rub in butter with fingertips until mixture resembles breadcrumbs. Stir in cream to make a pliable dough.
3 Shape dough into a ball, wrap in plastic film, and chill for 30 minutes. Roll out thinly.
4 With a pastry wheel or sharp knife, cut dough into squares or oblongs. Place on greased baking trays, allow room for spreading.
5 Bake at 200°C for 6-7 minutes, or until firm and golden brown. Cool for 2-3 minutes on trays. Transfer to a wire rack to cool completely. Store in an airtight container.

Caraway Twists

Preparation time:
  30 minutes
Cooking time:
  15 minutes
Makes about 50

2 eggs
²⁄₃ cup sugar
2½ teaspoons baking powder
½ cup vegetable oil
3 cups wholemeal plain flour, sifted
extra beaten egg white
caraway seeds

1 Beat two eggs until frothy. Gradually add sugar, then baking powder; beat 3 minutes. Add oil, beat 1 minute more. Add sifted flour gradually, stir until combined.
2 Roll tablespoonfuls of dough into long rope shapes about 10 cm in length. Fold in half and twist pieces together. Place on a greased baking tray. Brush with remaining beaten egg white. Sprinkle with caraway seeds.
3 Bake at 180°C for about 15 minutes, or until golden. Cool on trays for 2-3 minutes. Transfer to a wire rack. to cool completely. Store in an airtight container.

For Graham Crackers: rub butter into flour mixture until it resembles fine breadcrumbs.

Use a sharp, flat-bladed knife to cut biscuits into oblongs. Prick the top of each.

Cheese Shapes

Preparation time:
  30 minutes + chilling
Cooking time:
  5 minutes
Makes about 40

90 g butter
90 g *Cheddar cheese,*
  finely grated
3/4 cup plain flour, sifted
1/4 cup finely grated
  Parmesan cheese
1/2 teaspoon salt
1/4 teaspoon chilli
  powder (optional)
1 small egg, beaten
  chopped or flaked
  almonds

1 Beat butter in a small bowl until soft. Add Cheddar and mix well. Add sifted flour, Parmesan, salt and chilli powder. Mix to a soft dough, wrap and chill until firm, but not hard.
2 Roll out on a floured surface to a 3 mm thickness.
3 Coat dough twice with beaten egg. Sprinkle liberally with nuts, then cut with cocktail or sandwich-size cutters. Transfer shapes to a greased baking tray with a spatula. Allow room for spreading.
4 Bake at 180°C for about 5 minutes, or until lightly golden.

Cool on baking tray for 2-3 minutes. Transfer to a wire rack to cool completely. Store in an airtight container.

Note: These biscuits can be made a week or more in advance.

Spiced Biscuits

Preparation time:
  35 minutes
Cooking time:
  10 minutes
Makes about 40

1 1/2 *cups plain white or*
  wholemeal flour
1 teaspoon salt
1/4 teaspoon paprika
2 tablespoons butter
2 cups shredded
  Cheddar cheese
3 tablespoons water
2 teaspoons lemon juice
milk or cream for
  glazing
celery salt
extra shredded cheese,
  for topping

1 Sift flour, salt and paprika. Rub in butter with fingertips until mixture resembles breadcrumbs; mix in cheese.
2 Combine water and lemon juice. Stir in the dry ingredients, mixing to a stiff dough. Knead lightly.
3 On a floured surface, roll out dough thinly. Pierce well with a fork. Cut into squares or decorative shapes with a knife or cutters.
4 Place on a greased baking tray, allow room for spreading. Brush with milk. Sprinkle with celery salt and extra cheese.
5 Bake at 200°C for 10 minutes, or until golden. Cool on tray for 2-3 minutes. Transfer to a wire rack to cool completely. Store in an airtight container.

Oat Crackers

Preparation time:
  30 minutes
Cooking time:
  15 minutes
Makes about 25

2 cups rolled oats
1 cup plain flour
1 teaspoon baking
  powder
1 teaspoon salt
1/4 teaspoon mustard
  seeds
2 teaspoons curry
  powder
125 g *chilled butter,*
  chopped
1 cup grated Cheddar
  cheese
1 egg, *separated*

Back: Oat Crackers
Left: Cheese Shapes
Right: Spiced Biscuits

1 Process oats, flour, baking powder, salt, mustard seeds and curry powder until coarsely ground. Add butter and cheese and process until mixture resembles coarse breadcrumbs.
2 Add lightly beaten egg yolk and enough water to mix to a firm dough. Roll out on a lightly floured surface to 5 mm thickness. Cut dough into rounds or other shapes.
3 Brush a little beaten egg white over each. Place on a greased baking tray, allow room for spreading.
4 Bake at 190°C for 12-15 minutes, or until cooked. Cool the crackers on trays for 2-3 minutes. Transfer to a wire rack to cool completely. Store the crackers in an airtight container.

29

COOKIES

Cookies and biscuits are very similar. In the United States, the term 'cookie' is often used to describe any kind of biscuit; but the word derives from the Dutch *koekje* which means 'little cake'. Cookies are those scrumptious, melt-in-the-mouth confections that are usually not shaped with a biscuit cutter but dropped in teaspoonfuls onto a tray or shaped by hand into balls or rolled into log shapes and sliced to the desired thickness. They are often made from self-raising flour or plain flour and baking powder so the texture may be softer and lighter than that of a conventional biscuit.

When baking cookies, oven trays should be heavy and perfectly flat. If the recipe says to grease the tray, use unsalted butter, oil or a non-stick spray – and be sure to grease the whole area. When placing trays in the oven, make sure that heat can circulate all around them; check from time to time and turn trays to ensure even browning.

To store cookies: place the crisp kind in airtight containers. They can be freshened by heating briefly in a moderate oven. Soft cookies will keep their fresh-baked flavour and texture for some time if  you store them in an airtight container with a wedge of unpeeled apple. Replace the apple with a fresh wedge every day or so. In very humid weather, it's a good idea to store soft cookies in the refrigerator.

Basic Cookie Dough

Preparation time:
  25 minutes + chilling
Cooking time:
  15 minutes
Makes about 50

180 g butter
1¼ cups brown sugar
1 teaspoon imitation
  vanilla essence
1 egg
3 cups plain flour
1½ teaspoons baking
  powder

1 Beat butter and sugar in a small bowl with an electric mixer until light and fluffy. Add vanilla and egg; beat well. Sift flour and baking powder into creamed mixture. Mix well.
2 Divide mixture in half. Roll into a sausage shape (see Note) about 3 cm in diameter. Wrap each roll in plastic wrap. Refrigerate until firm (see Note).
3 Unwrap. Slice thinly using a sharp knife. Place on greased baking trays. Allow room for spreading. Bake at 180°C for 10-15 minutes, or until golden. Cool on trays for 2-3 minutes. Transfer to a wire rack to cool completely. Store in an airtight container.

Note: Dough may also be shaped into a square or triangular block. A ruler may be helpful to flatten sides. Also, dough could be cut into sticks or large rectangles when firm. Dough may be kept in the refrigerator for up to 1 week or frozen for up to 1 month. Just slice off the amount required.

Variations:
◆ Sultana Cookies: Add ½ cup sultanas in step 2.
◆ Cherry Cookies: Add ½ cup chopped glacé cherries in step 2.

*Basic Cookie with variations,
Choc-Mint Pin Wheels
& Cinnamon Swirls*

Choc-Mint Pin Wheels

Preparation time:
  35 minutes + chilling
Cooking time:
  15 minutes
Makes about 50

180 g butter
1¼ cups brown sugar
1 teaspoon imitation
  vanilla essence
1 egg
3 cups plain flour
1½ teaspoons baking
  powder
1 tablespoon cocoa
dash peppermint
  essence

1 Beat butter and sugar in a bowl with an electric mixer until light and fluffy. Beat in vanilla and egg. Sift flour and baking powder; mix well.
2 Divide mixture in half. Add cocoa to one half and peppermint essence to the other. Roll out each half of dough to form a rectangle 2 mm thick. Place the chocolate layer on a large sheet of greaseproof paper.
3 Place the peppermint layer on top of the chocolate layer. Roll up like a Swiss roll. Wrap in plastic film and refrigerate until firm.
4 Unwrap and slice thinly using a sharp knife. Place on greased baking trays. Bake at 180°C for 10-15 minutes or until golden. Cool on trays for 2-3 minutes.

Cinnamon Swirls

Preparation time:
  30 minutes + chilling
Cooking time:
  15 minutes
Makes about 50

180 g butter
1¼ cups brown sugar
1 teaspoon imitation
  vanilla essence
1 egg
3 cups plain flour
1½ teaspoons baking
  powder
2 teaspoons ground
  cinnamon
2 tablespoons caster
  sugar

1 Beat butter and sugar in a bowl with an electric mixer until light and fluffy. Beat in vanilla and egg. Sift the flour and baking powder; mix well. Roll out to form a rectangle 4mm thick.
2 Combine cinnamon and caster sugar and sprinkle over dough. Roll up like a Swiss roll. Wrap in plastic film and refrigerate until firm.
3 Unwrap and slice thinly. Place on greased baking trays. Bake at

For Choc-Mint Pin wheels: place peppermint layer on chocolate layer

Refrigerate until firm. Use a sharp, flat-bladed knife to slice into 2 cm rounds.

Ginger Jumbos

180°C for 10-15 minutes or until golden. Cool on trays. Transfer to a wire rack to cool completely. Store in an airtight container.

Ginger Jumbos

Preparation time:
  25 minutes
Cooking time:
  8 minutes
Makes about 35

2¼ *cups plain flour*
2 *teaspoons*
  bicarbonate of soda
1 *teaspoon ground*
  ginger
½ *teaspoon ground*
  cinnamon
¼ *teaspoon salt*
125 *g butter, softened*
⅓ *cup sugar*
⅓ *cup treacle*
⅓ *cup golden syrup*
1 *egg*
½ *cup milk*
1½ *teaspoons cider*
  vinegar
walnut pieces or peanut
  halves

1 Stir flour with bicarbonate of soda, spices and salt in a mixing bowl. Beat butter and sugar in a separate bowl with an electric mixer until light and fluffy. Beat in the treacle, golden syrup and egg.
2 Add dry ingredients, alternately with milk combined with the vinegar, stirring well each time.
3 Drop tablespoons of mixture onto greased baking trays, allow room for spreading. Top each with a walnut piece or half a peanut.
4 Bake at 200°C for 8 minutes, or until the centres spring back when lightly pressed. Cool on trays for 2-3 minutes. Transfer to a wire rack to cool completely. Store in an airtight container.

Lemon and Orange Drops

Preparation time:
  30 minutes
Cooking time:
  15 minutes
Makes about 30

125 g butter
2 teaspoons grated
  orange rind
¾ cup sugar
1 egg, lightly beaten
1 cup plain flour, sifted
½ cup self-raising flour,
  sifted
2 tablespoons orange
  juice
¾ cup desiccated
  coconut

Orange topping
1 cup icing sugar, sifted
2 teaspoons water
2 teaspoons orange juice
1 teaspoon each grated
  orange and lemon rind

1 Beat butter, orange
rind and sugar in a
small bowl with an
electric mixer until
creamy. Add egg and
mix well. Fold in sifted
flours. Add orange juice
and coconut and mix
until well combined.
2 Drop level
tablespoonfuls of
mixture onto greased
baking trays. Bake at
180°C for 12-15
minutes, or until
golden. While still
warm, spread the

topping over and
sprinkle with grated
orange rind if you wish.
3 To make topping:
combine sifted icing
sugar, water and orange
juice until smooth.
Sprinkle over orange
and lemon rind. Store
in an airtight container.

Chewy Orange Cookies

Preparation time:
  20 minutes
Cooking time:
  12 minutes
Makes about 35

⅔ cup raw sugar
2 tablespoons
  polyunsaturated oil
1 egg white
3 tablespoons fresh or
  unsweetened orange
  juice
2 teaspoons grated
  orange peel
1½ cups self-raising
  flour, sifted
2 tablespoons currants

1 Combine sugar and
oil in bowl. Beat egg
white, orange juice and
peel. Fold in sifted flour
and currants.

*Left to right:
Chocolate Chip
Cookies, Lemon
and Orange Drops
& Chewy Orange
Cookies*

2 Drop two
teaspoonfuls onto a
lightly floured baking
tray, allow room for
spreading. Bake at
180°C for 10-12
minutes, or until

HINT
Cookies always seem soft when removed from
the oven – they often taste best like this. After
cooking and cooling, cookies become crisper.
Store crisp cookies in an airtight container.

browned. Serve warm
or cold.
Store in an airtight
container.

Chocolate Chip Cookies

Preparation time:
  20 minutes
Cooking time:
  12 minutes
Makes about 35

185 g butter, softened
½ cup caster sugar
¼ cup brown sugar
1 egg
1 teaspoon imitation
  vanilla essence
1¾ cups self-raising
  flour, sifted
1 cup pecans or
  walnuts, chopped
1 cup chocolate bits

1 Beat butter, sugars,
egg and vanilla essence
in a small bowl with an
electric mixer until soft
and creamy. Stir in
sifted flour, nuts and
chocolate bits.
2 Drop tablespoonfuls
onto greased baking
trays, allow room for
spreading. Bake at
180°C for 10-12
minutes, or until golden
brown. Cool on trays
for 2-3 minutes.
Transfer to a wire rack.
Cool completely. Store
in an airtight container.

Coconut Drops &
Marshmallow Cookies

Coconut Drops

Preparation time:
  20 minutes
Cooking time:
  15 minutes
Makes about 40

1 cup plain flour
1/2 teaspoon baking
  powder
125 g butter
1/3 cup caster sugar
1/2 teaspoon imitation
  vanilla essence
2 tablespoons orange
  juice
2 eggs, beaten
2/3 cup desiccated
  coconut
1/3 cup chocolate bits
1/3 cup shredded coconut

1 Sift flour and baking powder into a bowl. Rub in butter with fingertips until mixture resembles breadcrumbs. Add remaining ingredients and mix thoroughly.
2 Drop two teaspoonfuls of mixture onto greased

HINT
Allow hot cookies to stand for at least 1 minute on their baking tray after cooking. Transfer them to a wire rack to cool completely and avoid sweating.

baking trays. Allow room for spreading. Bake at 190°C for 10-15 minutes, or until golden. Cool on trays for 2-3 minutes. Transfer to wire rack. Store in an airtight container.

HINT
Butter gives a better texture and flavour to cookies than margarine, so we have specified butter in our recipes.

Marshmallow Cookies

Preparation time:
  50 minutes
Cooking time:
  15 minutes
Makes about 45

1 cup brown sugar
1 egg
2 cups self-raising flour,
  sifted
2 tablespoons cocoa,
  sifted
125 g butter
3 tablespoons milk
grated chocolate

Marshmallow
1/2 cup sugar
2 teaspoons gelatine
6 tablespoons water
1 teaspoon imitation
  vanilla essence
red food colouring

1 Combine brown sugar, egg and half the sifted flour and cocoa in a mixing bowl. Melt butter over gentle heat; stir in milk. Pour over dry ingredients. Beat for 2-3 minutes. Add remaining flour and cocoa; mix thoroughly.
2 Roll small portions of mixture into balls. Place on greased baking trays, allow room for spreading. Flatten the top of each cookie with a fork. Bake at 180°C for 15 minutes, or until golden. Cool on trays for 2-3 minutes. Transfer to a wire rack to cool completely.
3 To make the marshmallow: combine the sugar, gelatine and water in a small pan over low heat until mixture boils. Simmer for 3-4 minutes, then cool. Stir in vanilla essence and colour pink. Beat until thick and fluffy.
4 When cookies are cold, spoon over marshmallow. Decorate with grated chocolate. Store in an airtight container.

Note: Do not top with marshmallow until the day the biscuits are to be eaten, as they will soften.

Munchy Oatmeals

Preparation time:
  25 minutes
Cooking time:
  8 minutes
Makes about 40

125 g butter, softened
¹⁄₂ cup caster sugar
¹⁄₂ cup brown sugar
2 teaspoons imitation
  vanilla essence
2 eggs
³⁄₄ cup plain flour
¹⁄₂ teaspoon salt
¹⁄₄ teaspoon
  bicarbonate of soda
2 cups rolled oats
¹⁄₄ cup chopped
  hazlenuts

1 Beat butter, sugars
and vanilla in a large
bowl with an electric
mixer until light and
fluffy. Add the eggs and
beat well.
2 Sift flour, salt and
soda into creamed
mixture. Fold in
1¹⁄₂ cups of oats and
the hazelnuts.
3 Roll heaped
teaspoonfuls of mixture
in remaining oats. Place
onto greased baking
trays. Allow room for
spreading. Bake at
180°C for 8 minutes, or
until golden brown.
Cool on trays for 2-3
minutes. Transfer to a
wire rack to cool. Store
in an airtight container.

Chocolate Cookies

Preparation time:
  25 minutes
Cooking time:
  15 minutes
Makes about 30

125 g butter
¹⁄₃ cup caster sugar
2 tablespoons
  condensed milk
1 teaspoon imitation
  vanilla essence
1 cup self-raising flour,
  sifted
120 g cooking
  chocolate, grated

1 Beat butter and sugar
in a small bowl with an
electric mixer until light
and fluffy. Beat in
condensed milk and
vanilla essence. Fold in
sifted flours and grated
chocolate.
2 Drop two
teaspoonfuls of mixture
onto greased baking
trays, allow room for
spreading. Bake at
160°C for 15 minutes,
or until golden. Cool on
trays for 2-3 minutes.
Transfer to a wire rack
to cool completely. Store
in an airtight container.

Note: Drizzle chocolate
cookies with melted
white and dark
chocolate, if desired.
Always heat chocolate
gently over indirect heat
or hot water.

Clockwise from box: Peanut-Frosted Brownies, Munchy Oatmeals,
Chocolate Cookies, Brandy Currant Cookies & Fruit Delights

For Peanut-Frosted Brownies: beat butter and sugar, add eggs and vanilla; mix.

Fold dry ingredients into butter and stir in chopped peanuts.

Peanut-Frosted Brownies

Preparation time:
  35 minutes
Cooking time:
  30 minutes
Makes about 25

1 cup plain flour
1/2 cup cocoa
1/2 teaspoon baking
  powder
1/4 teaspoon salt
125 g butter, softened
1 1/2 cups brown sugar
3 eggs
1 teaspoon imitation
  vanilla essence
1/2 cup unsalted
  peanuts, chopped

Peanut Butter Frosting
60 g butter
1 cup icing sugar, sifted
1/4 cup peanut butter
1 tablespoon boiling
  water

1 Sift flour, cocoa, baking powder and salt into a bowl. Beat butter and sugar in a small bowl with an electric mixer until light and fluffy. Add eggs and vanilla; mix well. Fold in dry ingredients and peanuts; combine thoroughly.
2 Spoon into a greased 28 x 18 cm shallow oblong baking tin. Bake at 180°C for 30 minutes, or until cooked. Cool in the tin. When cold, spread with frosting.
3 To make frosting: beat butter and sifted icing sugar until creamy. Combine peanut butter with water and stir into mixture until smooth. Spread over brownies. Store in an airtight container, in the refrigerator in warmer weather.

Brandy Currant Cookies

Preparation time:
  25 minutes + 2 hours
  soaking and chilling
Cooking time:
  10 minutes
Makes about 45

1 cup currants
1/3 cup brandy, heated
250 g butter
1 cup sugar
1 whole egg
1 egg yolk
1/2 teaspoon ground
  nutmeg
1 teaspoon ground
  cinnamon
2 1/2 cups plain flour,
  sifted

1 Soak the currants in brandy for 1 hour. Drain, reserving brandy.
2 Beat butter and sugar in a bowl until light and

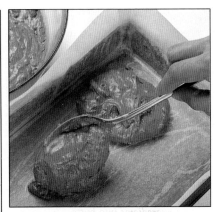

Spoon the mixture into a lined and greased shallow oblong baking tin.

Use a spatula to spread mixture evenly over baking tin.

fluffy. Add egg, egg yolk and spices; mix well. Stir in 2 teaspoons reserved brandy with currants. Combine with sifted flour to make a smooth dough. Wrap in plastic film and chill for 1 hour.

3 Roll tablespoonfuls into balls. Place on greased baking trays, allow room for spreading. Flatten the top of each cookie with a fork.

4 Bake at 180°C for 10 minutes, or until pale golden. Cool on trays for 2-3 minutes. Transfer to a wire rack to cool. Store in an airtight container.

Note. For non-drinkers, dried fruits can be plumped up by soaking in tea. Whisky or marsala also give a good flavour to dried fruit.

Fruit Delights

Preparation time:
  30 minutes
Cooking time:
  12 minutes
Makes about 65

185 g butter
1 cup brown sugar
1 cup caster sugar
2 eggs, beaten
½ teaspoon
  bicarbonate of soda
½ cup sour cream
3½ cups plain flour
¼ cup cornflour
1 teaspoon imitation
  vanilla essence
1 cup chopped raisins
½ cup chopped mixed
  peel
1 cup glacé cherries
1 cup blanched
  almonds, chopped

1 Beat butter and sugars in a bowl with an electric mixer until creamy. Add eggs and beat well. Stir soda into cream, let dissolve and stir into creamed mixture; mix well.

2 Sift together flours. Stir half into creamed mixture. Add vanilla essence, raisins, peel, cherries and nuts; mix thoroughly. Fold in remaining flour and mix well.

3 Drop teaspoonfuls of mixture onto greased baking trays, allow room for spreading. Bake at 180°C for about 12 minutes, or until golden. Cool on trays for 2-3 minutes. Transfer to a wire rack to cool completely.

Lemon-Nutmeg Stars

Preparation time:
 35 minutes
Cooking time:
 15 minutes
Makes about 25

1 cup self-raising flour,
 sifted
1/2 cup cornflour
1/4 teaspoon salt
1/2 teaspoon ground
 nutmeg
155 g butter, softened
1/2 cup icing sugar
2 teaspoons finely
 grated lemon rind
1/2 cup apricot preserve
icing sugar

1 Sift flour, cornflour, salt and nutmeg into a bowl. Beat butter, icing sugar and lemon rind in a bowl until light and fluffy. Add dry ingredients and beat, scraping the bowl, until the mixture is smooth.
2 Roll dough out to 3 mm thickness. Cut dough into 50 stars using a small fluted cutter, cut out centre of 25 stars using a smaller fluted cutter.
3 Place on lightly greased baking trays. Bake at 150°C for 15 minutes, or until very pale golden around the edges. Cool for 2-3 minutes on trays. Transfer to a wire rack

to cool completely.
4 Heat apricot preserve in a small pan for 2 minutes, stirring constantly. Leave to cool before using just enough to hold cookies together firmly. Sandwich stars together with jam. Dust with icing sugar.

Pecan Buttons

Preparation time:
 20 minutes
Cooking time:
 25 minutes
Makes about 20

125 g butter, softened
1/2 cup sugar
1 egg yolk
1/2 teaspoon almond
 essence
1 cup self-raising flour,
 sifted
1/2 cup chopped pecans
pecan halves

1 Beat butter and sugar in a bowl with an electric mixer until light and fluffy. Add egg yolk and almond essence; mix well. Stir in sifted flour and chopped pecans. Chill mixture for 30 minutes.
2 Shape tablespoonfuls of dough into balls. Place on greased baking trays, allow room for spreading. Press a pecan half in the centre top of each cookie.

3 Bake at 150°C for 25 minutes, or until lightly browned. Cool on trays for 2-3 minutes. Transfer to a wire rack to cool completely. Store in an airtight container.

Raspberry Cookies

Preparation time:
 25 minutes
Cooking time:
 12 minutes
Makes about 25

250 g butter
1/4 cup caster sugar
1 teaspoon almond
 essence
2 cups plain flour, sifted
sesame seeds
raspberry jam

1 Beat butter and sugar in a bowl with an electric mixer until light and fluffy. Gradually stir in almond essence and sifted flour. Shape tablespoonfuls of dough into balls and roll in sesame seeds.
2 Place on ungreased baking trays and flatten slightly with a fork. Make a hollow in the centre of each with the end of a wooden spoon handle and fill with 1/2 teaspoon of jam.
3 Bake at 190°C for 10-12 minutes, or until done. Cool on trays for 2-3 minutes. Transfer to

*Clockwise from left: Pecan Buttons,
Raspberry Cookies, Lemon-Nutmeg Stars*

a wire rack to cool
completely. Store in an
airtight container, with
plastic wrap between
the layers, in a cool,
dry place.

HINT
Cookies filled with jam or icing should be eaten
soon after filling. If you want to make them
ahead of time, leave filling until serving.

Finnish Cookies

Preparation time:
  30 minutes + 1 hour
  chilling
Cooking time:
  12 minutes
Makes about 24

250 g butter
1/2 cup sugar
1 teaspoon almond
  essence
1 2/3 cups plain flour,
  sifted
1/2 cup blanched
  almonds, finely
  chopped
3 tablespoons extra
  sugar
1 egg yolk
1 tablespoon water
60 g plain dark
  chocolate, chopped
2 teaspoons butter

1 Beat butter, sugar
and almond essence in a
bowl with an electric
mixer until light and
fluffy. Mix in sifted
flour to form a soft
dough. Wrap in
greaseproof paper and
chill for at least 1 hour.
2 Combine almonds
and the extra sugar.
Beat egg yolk and water
until blended. Shape 2
teaspoons of dough into
8 cm long, narrow
fingers.
3 Brush with egg
mixture. Dip tops in
nut mixture and place
on ungreased baking
trays, allow room for
spreading.
4 Bake at 180°C for
12 minutes, or until
golden. Cool on trays
for 2-3 minutes.
Transfer to a wire rack
to cool completely.
5 If desired, melt
chopped chocolate and
butter in a small pan
over low heat. Cool
slightly and then drizzle
over cold cookies.

Walnut Pinwheels

Preparation time:
  40 minutes +
  overnight chilling time
  and 1 hour standing
Cooking time:
  15 minutes
Makes about 35

250 g butter
250 g creamed cheese
1/4 cup sour cream
2 1/4 cups plain flour,
  sifted

Filling
2 cups ground or finely
  chopped walnuts
1/2 cup sugar
1 teaspoon ground
  cinnamon
1 egg
1 teaspoon grated
  orange rind

1 Beat butter and
cream cheese in a bowl
with an electric mixer
until creamy. Beat in the
sour cream. Add the
sifted flour; mix to a
form dough, adding a
little more flour, if
necessary. Form into a
ball, wrap in
greaseproof paper and
chill overnight.
2 To make filling:
combine walnuts, sugar,
cinnamon, egg and
orange rind. Divide
dough in half, roll out
one half on a floured
surface to a square
about 5 mm thick.
Spread half the filling
evenly over, roll up as
for a Swiss roll. Wrap
in foil, chill for at least
1 hour. Repeat with the
other half of the dough.
3 Cut the rolls into
5 mm thick slices. Place
on the greased baking
trays, re-shaping them
into rounds, and allow
room for spreading.
4 Bake at 180°C for
15 minutes, or until
firm and golden. Cool
on trays for 2-3
minutes. Transfer to a
wire rack to cool
completely. Store in an
airtight container.

Coffee Shapes

Preparation time:
  30 minutes
Cooking time:
  15 minutes
Makes about 30

Clockwise from top: Finnish Cookies, Coffee Shapes & Walnut Pinwheels

60 g butter
1/4 cup caster sugar
1 egg
2 tablespoons milk
1 1/2 cups plain flour
1/4 teaspoon baking powder
2 1/2 teaspoons instant coffee powder
chopped nuts to decorate

Coffee icing
1 1/4 cups icing sugar, sifted
2 teaspoons instant coffee powder
1 tablespoon water

1 Beat butter and sugar in a bowl with an electric mixer until light and fluffy. Add egg and milk; beat well.
2 Sift together flour, baking powder and coffee. Stir dry ingredients into creamed mixture to form a dough; knead lightly.
3 Roll out thinly on a floured board. Cut into desired shapes with floured cutters. Place on greased baking trays, allow room for spreading.
4 Bake at 180°C for 15 minutes, or until light brown. Cool on trays for 2-3 minutes.

Transfer to a wire rack to cool completely. When cold, top with icing and sprinkle with the nuts (or dip iced biscuits into chopped nuts, if preferred.)
5 To make icing: combine all ingredients in a small pan. Stir over a low heat until lukewarm and a thick spreading consistency. Remove from heat; stand pan in a larger pan of hot water to keep mixture spreadable while using. Cover biscuits with icing and decorate with nuts. Store in an airtight container.

45

Yoghurt and Lemon Cookies

Preparation time:
  20 minutes
Cooking time:
  12 minutes
Makes about 60

150 g unsalted butter
1½ cups caster sugar
1 tablespoon grated
  lemon rind
2 teaspoons lemon juice
2 eggs
2 cups plain flour
½ cup cornflour
½ teaspoon
  bicarbonate of soda
2 tablespoons plain
  yoghurt

1 Beat butter, sugar and lemon rind until light and fluffy, add lemon juice, mix well. Add eggs one at a time, beat well to combine.
2 Stir sifted flour, cornflour and soda into creamed mixture, stir in yoghurt, mix well.
3 Place two teaspoonfuls of mixture onto greased baking trays, allow room for spreading. Bake for 10-12 minutes or until lightly golden. Cool on trays for 2-3 minutes, transfer to wire rack to cool completely.

Note: These cookies can be spread with lemon icing if desired.

HINT
Do not over-grease baking trays. Too much greasing will result in cookies becoming too dark underneath while baking. Grease trays lightly with melted butter, non-stick spray or line with baking paper.

HINT
In some humid climates or in a kitchen with too high a temperature your cookie, biscuit or shortbread mixture could be a little soft. You may need to incorporate a little more flour into the mixture. In some instances refrigerate the mixture for about 20 minutes, wrapped in plastic film, to achieve a good working consistency. In colder climates and cool kitchens a little more liquid may be added.

Apricot Coconut Cookies

Preparation time:
  20 minutes
Cooking time:
  15 minutes
Makes about 50

3 eggs
1 cup caster sugar
60 g butter
1 tablespoon grated
  orange rind
1 tablespoon orange
  juice
½ cup chopped dried
  apricots
2 cups rolled oats
¼ cup self-raising flour
1 cup desiccated
  coconut

1 Beat eggs, sugar, butter, orange rind and orange juice until light and fluffy.
2 Fold in apricots, rolled oats, sifted flour and coconut, mix well to combine.
3 Drop two teaspoonfuls of mixture onto greased baking trays, allow room for spreading. Bake at 180°C for 12-15 minutes or until lightly golden. Cool on trays for 2-3 minutes. Transfer to a wire rack to cool completely.

Left: Apricot Coconut Cookies. Right: Yoghurt and Lemon Cookies

SHORTBREAD

One homemade gift idea that never seems to go amiss is shortbread. Often reserved for Christmas celebrations, you can of course make and enjoy it all year round. There are many versions of this treat. Despite being traditionally associated with Scotland, there are English, Greek and German recipes, and many delicious modern variations as well.

Use your imagination when shaping shortbread dough. Bake it in square or round tins, use wooden moulds or cut it into patterns with biscuit cutters to suit the season and delight your family and friends. Decorative moulds and biscuit cutters are available in a wonderful variety of shapes and forms, and are great fun to experiment with.

Store shortbread as for cookies and biscuits, in an airtight container. It helps to wrap shortbread in waxed paper before putting it in a biscuit tin – this will keep it fresher for longer. Shortbread will keep for up to four weeks.

Oat Shortbread

Brown sugar adds rich colour and flavour to shortbread, while the oats give it a slightly different texture and lots of crunch!

Preparation time:
  20 minutes + 20 minutes chilling
Cooking time:
  15-20 minutes
Makes about 48

250 g butter, softened
3/4 cup brown sugar
2 teaspoons imitation vanilla essence
2 cups plain flour, sifted
1 cup rolled oats

1 Beat butter, sugar and vanilla essence in a bowl with an electric mixer until creamy. Gradually blend in sifted flour and oats using a wooden spoon, then your hands, if necessary. Wrap and chill the dough for about 20 minutes.
2 On a floured surface, roll the dough to about a 5 mm thickness. Cut into small rounds, bars or other shapes with cutters, as desired.
3 Place on ungreased baking trays and pierce well with a fork. Bake at 160°C for 15-20 minutes, or until firm and golden. Cool on trays for 2-3 minutes.

Transfer to a wire rack to cool completely. Store in an airtight container.

Hazelnut Shortbread

Preparation time:
  30 minutes + chilling
Cooking time:
  15 minutes
Makes about 30

250 g butter, softened
1/2 cup sugar
1 egg, plus 1 egg yolk, extra
1 teaspoon imitation vanilla essence
1 1/2 cups plain flour
1/2 teaspoon baking powder
1/4 teaspoon bicarbonate of soda
1/2 cup finely ground hazelnuts
about 30 whole hazelnuts

1 Beat butter and sugar in a bowl with an electric mixer until light and fluffy. Beat in egg, egg yolk and vanilla. Sift in flour, baking powder and soda. Add ground hazelnuts and mix well.
2 Lightly roll level tablespoonfuls of mixture into rounds, place on greased baking trays, allow room for spreading. Flatten slightly and place a whole hazelnut on each.

Front: Hazelnut Shortbread. Back: Oat Shortbread

3 Bake at 180°C for 12-15 minutes, or until just lightly golden. Cool on trays for 2-3 minutes. Transfer to a wire rack to cool completely.

Traditional Shortbread

This is based on the old-fashioned recipe. It's perfectly acceptable to replace some of the plain flour with rice flour for a finer texture.

Preparation time:
  20 minutes
Cooking time:
  40 minutes
Makes about 8 wedges

250 g butter, softened
1/2 cup icing sugar, sifted
12/3 cups plain flour
1/4 cup rice flour

1 Beat butter and icing sugar in a bowl with an electric mixer until light and fluffy. Sift in flours; combine well with a wooden spoon.
2 Press dough into a ball; knead lightly until smooth. Pat dough into a 23 cm round tin, or into a 23 cm round, about 1 cm thick, on greased baking tray.
3 Score into fingers or wedges. Pierce with fork. Bake at 140°C for 35-40 minutes, or until set and browned.
4 Cool on trays for 2-3 minutes. Transfer to a wire rack. When almost cool, cut through lines into pieces (try using a bread knife in a sawing motion for neat pieces). Cool shortbread completely. Store in an airtight container.

Note: Dough can be rolled out and cut into small rounds or bars, cut with scone or biscuit cutters, or pressed into wooden shortbread or butter moulds, as desired. Reduce baking times if cooking smaller pieces.

Almond Shortbread Biscuits

Preparation time:
  25 minutes + 30 minutes chilling
Cooking time:
  12 minutes
Makes about 36

125 g butter
1/3 cup caster sugar
1 teaspoon imitation almond essence
1 egg yolk
3/4 cup plain flour, sifted
1/4 cup rice flour, sifted
1/2 cup self-raising flour, sifted
60 g blanched almonds

1 Beat butter and sugar in a bowl with an electric mixer until light

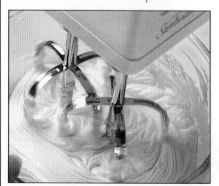

For Traditional Shortbread: beat butter and icing sugar together until light and fluffy.

Fold sifted flour into butter mixture using a wooden spoon.

Traditional Shortbread

Pinch a decorative edge to shortbread round, using floured fingers as shown.

Score into wedges (or fingers) and pierce with a fork.

Almond Shortbread Biscuits

Cherry Almond Squares

Preparation time:
  25 minutes
Cooking time:
  35 minutes
Makes about 24

2 cups plain flour, sifted
1/2 cup icing sugar, sifted
250 g butter, chopped

Topping
30 g butter
1/3 cup caster sugar
2 teaspoons imitation
  vanilla essence
1 tablespoon milk
125 g blanched
  almonds, halved
125 g glacé cherries,
  chopped

1 Place flour and icing sugar into a bowl. Rub in butter with fingertips until mixture resembles breadcrumbs.
2 Press into a greased 18 x 28 cm shallow oblong baking tin. Bake at 200°C for 15 minutes, or until lightly golden brown.
3 To make topping: melt butter in a pan.

and fluffy. Add almond essence and egg yolk; beat well.
2 Stir in flours. Mix to a firm dough. Roll into a log shape. Cover with plastic wrap. Refrigerate for 30 minutes.
3 Slice the dough into 3 mm rounds. Place on a greased baking tray, allow room for spreading. Press an almond on top of each round.
4 Bake at 180°C for 12 minutes. Cool on tray for 2-3 minutes. Transfer to a wire rack to cool completely. Store in an airtight container.

HINT
For better shaping, add a little water to your dough mixture then allow about 5 minutes standing time for the dough to absorb it before shaping. Be careful not to add too much!

HINT
Rice flour or ground flour usually feature in traditional recipes. The amount of rice flour used may vary from recipe to recipe, but its function is to add a certain 'sandiness' to the texture; If you enjoy this add a little more rice flour, a little less plain flour to your shortbread.

Cherry Almond Squares

Stir in sugar, vanilla essence and milk. Do not stir continuously. Mix in almonds. Allow to cool.
4 Fold in cherries. Spread over partly cooked base. Bake at 200°C for 15-20 minutes, or until almonds are golden. Cool in tin. Cut into

squares and serve. Store in an airtight container.

Note: The topping mixture may crystallise if stirred too much after the sugar is added.

HINT
Shortbread shapes, e.g. Christmas trees, angels and bells, can be made with a hole in the top, so you can thread through some pretty ribbon and use them as Christmas tree ornaments.

Spitzbuben

Preparation time:
  30 minutes
Cooking time:
  10 minutes
Makes about 16

155 g butter
1/3 cup sugar
1 1/2 cups plain flour
1/2 teaspoon baking
  powder
1/3 cup finely chopped
  blanched almonds
1 teaspoon imitation
  vanilla essence
2 teaspoons rum
strawberry or raspberry
  jam
icing sugar, sifted

1 Beat butter and sugar
in a bowl with an
electric mixer until
creamy. Sift in flour and
baking powder; mix
well. Add almonds,
vanilla essence and
rum; mix to a dough.
2 Wrap in greaseproof
paper and refrigerate
until firm enough to
roll out. Roll into a
round and cut with a
fluted cutter 5 cm in
diameter. Using a
smaller fluted cutter, cut
the centres from half of
the rounds to form
rings.
3 Place larger rounds
and rings on the
greased baking trays
and bake at 190°C for
10 minutes, or until

they are golden. Cool
on trays for 2-3
minutes. Transfer to a
wire rack to cool
completely.
4 When cold, spread
the jam on whole
rounds, top with rings
and dust with sifted
icing sugar. Store in an
airtight container.

Raspberry Fingers

Preparation time:
  30 minutes
Cooking time:
  45 minutes
Makes about 15

125 g butter
3/4 cup caster sugar
2 eggs, separated
1 cup self-raising flour,
  sifted
1/2 cup plain flour, sifted
3 tablespoons raspberry
  jam
extra 1/2 cup caster sugar
1/2 cup desiccated
  coconut

1 Beat butter and sugar
in a bowl with an
electric mixer until light
and fluffy. Add egg
yolks; mix well. Fold in
sifted flours and mix to
a soft dough.
2 Press mixture into a
greased 28 x 18 cm
shallow oblong baking
tin. Spread with jam.
Beat egg whites until

soft peaks form.
Gradually beat in extra
sugar and continue
beating until stiff. Fold
in coconut; spread
mixture over jam.
3 Bake at 180°C for
45 minutes, or until
cooked. Cool in the tin.
When cold, cut into
fingers and serve.
Store in an airtight
container.

Clockwise from top right: Raspberry Fingers, Spitzbuben & Ginger Shortbread

Ginger Shortbread

Preparation time:
  25 minutes
Cooking time:
  45 minutes
Makes about 36

250 g butter, softened
1/2 cup icing sugar, sifted
2 cups plain flour, sifted
1 teaspoon ground
  ginger
1/3 cup chopped
  crystallised ginger

1 Heat butter and sugar in a bowl with an electric mixer until light and fluffy. Fold in sifted flour and gingers; mix well.
2 Press dough into a ball. Knead until smooth. Pat dough into an ungreased 23 cm square tin or shape into a round about 1 cm thick on a baking tray. Pierce well with a fork. Score into fingers or wedges.
3 Bake at 150°C for 40-45 minutes, or until lightly browned. While still warm, cut into wedges. Cool on tray for 2-3 minutes.

Left: Greek Shortbread. Plate:
Chocolate Shortbread & Wholemeal Nut Triangles

Greek Shortbread

Preparation time:
  20 minutes
Cooking time:
  15 minutes
Makes about 60

250 g unsalted butter
½ cup caster sugar
1 egg yolk
¼ teaspoon ground
  cloves
½ teaspoon imitation
  vanilla essence
⅓ cup brandy or ouzo
⅓ teaspoon
  bicarbonate of soda,
  dissolved in 1
  tablespoon lemon juice
½ cup toasted almonds,
  finely chopped
4 cups flour, sifted
icing sugar, sifted

1 Beat butter and sugar
in a bowl with an
electric mixer until light
and fluffy. Add egg
yolk, ground cloves,
vanilla essence, brandy
and the soda and lemon
juice mixture; mix well.
2 Fold in almonds and
sifted flour. Roll two
tablespoons of mixture
into sausage shapes.

Form into oval shapes.
Place on ungreased
baking tray.
3 Bake at 150°C for
15 minutes, or until
lightly browned.
Loosen from tray and
cool for 5 minutes.
Transfer to a wire rack
to cool completely. Dust
with sifted icing sugar.
Store in an airtight
container.

Wholemeal Nut Triangles

Preparation time:
  25 minutes
Cooking time:
  40 minutes
Makes about 24

1½ cups wholemeal
  flour, sifted
½ cup plain white
  flour, sifted
¼ cup ground almonds
⅓ cup brown sugar
½ teaspoon grated
  lemon rind
185 g softened butter,
  chopped
½ cup blanched
  almonds, chopped

HINT

Most shortbread recipes in this book can be
shaped as individual biscuits or as a 'round'.
Cooking times for a larger round will be longer,
so just use your common sense and keep
checking until shortbread turns a pale golden
brown, when it will be cooked.

1 Combine sifted flours, ground almonds, sugar and peel in a bowl, mix well. Rub in butter with fingertips until mixture resembles breadcrumbs. Knead gently to form a soft dough. Divide in half.
2 Firmly press each portion into a 20 cm fluted flan tin with a removable base. Smooth surfaces and pierce well with a fork. Score into wedges. Sprinkle almonds over the top and press lightly.
3 Bake at 180°C for 15 minutes. Reduce temperature to 150°C and bake a further 25 minutes, or until golden. Cool in tin for 2-3 minutes. While still warm, cut into wedges. Transfer to a wire rack to cool completely. Store in an airtight container.

> **HINT**
> Always use butter rather than margarine. You *can* make shortbread with margarine, but butter seems to hold the mixture together better.

> **HINT**
> Vanilla sugar is available in small jars. If you would like to make your own, buy some vanilla beans from a health food store, push 2-3 beans into a jar of caster sugar and leave for a few weeks to flavour the sugar.

Chocolate Shortbread

Sure to please both chocoholics and shortbread fanatics, these biscuits can be left plain or decorated with melted chocolate.

Preparation time:
  20 minutes
Cooking time:
  25 minutes
Makes about 50

250 g butter, softened
1 cup icing sugar, sifted
1 teaspoon imitation
  vanilla essence
2 cups plain flour, sifted
1/2 cup cocoa, sifted

1 Beat butter and sugar in a bowl with an electric mixer until light and fluffy. Mix in vanilla. Fold in sifted flour and cocoa; mix well.
2 Press dough into a ball. On a floured surface, roll out dough to a 5 mm thickness. Cut into fingers, small rounds or other shapes.
3 Place on greased baking trays. Pierce well with a fork. Bake at 150°C for about 25

minutes, or until firm and brown. Cool on trays for 2-3 minutes. Transfer to a wire rack to cool completely. Decorate as desired before serving.

Cherry Shortbread Slice

Preparation time:
  20 minutes
Cooking time:
  35 minutes
Makes about 24

Cherry Shortbread Slice

1¾ cup plain flour
½ cup icing sugar
2½ tablespoons cocoa
250 g butter, cubed

Topping
30 g butter
⅓ cup caster sugar
1 tablespoon milk
1 teaspoon imitation
  vanilla essence
⅓ cup sultanas
100 g glacé cherries,
  chopped
¼ cup walnuts, chopped

1 Sift flour, icing sugar and cocoa together into a bowl. Add butter. Rub in using your fingertips, until the mixture resembles coarse breadcrumbs.
2 Press lightly into a greased 18 x 28 cm shallow oblong baking tray. Bake at 200°C for 15 minutes.
3 To prepare topping: Melt butter in a small saucepan. Stir in sugar, milk and vanilla. Remove from heat. Stir in fruit and nuts. Cool slightly.

4 Spread over base. Bake at 180°C for 15-20 minutes. Cut into squares or fingers. Store in an airtight container.

> **HINT**
> If making tradional Scottish shortbread as a gift, wrap in Cellophane with a piece of tartan ribbon or present in a tartan-patterned box for an authentic Scottish feel.

Quick Shortbread

Preparation time:
  10 minutes
Cooking time:
  60 minutes
Makes about 30

2 cups plain flour
½ cup icing sugar
250 g cold butter, cut
  into 8 pieces
caster sugar

1 Measure flour and icing sugar into your food processor container; process a few seconds to mix.
2 Add butter pieces; process, turning On and Off until mixture forms fine crumbs, about 30 seconds. Then process continually until mixture clumps on to the blades. Stop the processor.
3 Turn into a 23 cm square baking tin. Shape into a ball, then press evenly into tin. Pierce well with fork. Score into wedges.
4 Bake at 150°C for 50-60 minutes, or until firm and lightly browned. Remove from oven and sprinkle lightly with caster sugar.
5 While still warm, cut into wedges. Cool in tin for 2-3 minutes. Transfer to a wire rack to cool completely. Store in an airtight container.

Almond Squares

Preparation time:
  25 minutes
Cooking time:
  50 minutes
Makes about 16

1¼ cups plain flour,
  sifted
½ cup caster sugar
125 g butter

Filling
½ cup ground almonds
2 tablespoons sugar
60 g butter
1 egg
2 teaspoons grated
  lemon rind
1 tablespoon plain flour

1 Combine sifted flour and sugar in a bowl. Rub in butter with fingertips until mixture resembles breadcrumbs. Press half over the base of a 20 cm square baking tin; reserve the other half. Bake at 180°C for 10 minutes. Remove and set aside to cool slightly.
2 To make filling: beat ground almonds, sugar and butter in a bowl until creamy. Add egg, lemon rind and flour; mix well. Spread filling over partially cooked base. Sprinkle over reserved flour mixture and press down lightly.
3 Bake at 180°C for 35-40 minutes, or until

*Quick Shortbread,
Almond Squares*

topping is golden brown and filling is firm. Cool in tin then cut into squares to serve. If you wish, decorate with blanched almonds half-covered with melted chocolate.

Austrian Crescents

Preparation time:
  25 minutes + chilling
Cooking time:
  12 minutes
Makes about 30

220 g butter
1/3 cup caster sugar
2 teaspoons finely
  grated lemon rind
2 1/4 cups plain flour,
  sifted
185 g ground almonds
1 teaspoon imitation
  vanilla essence
vanilla sugar

1 Beat butter and sugar in a bowl with an electric mixer until creamy. Beat in lemon rind. Fold in sifted flour, ground almonds and vanilla essence. Mix to form a soft dough. Wrap in greaseproof paper and chill until firm.
2 Shape into rolls as thick as a thumb and cut into 2.5 cm sections. Form these again into 5 cm long rolls and shape into crescents.

3 Place on greased baking trays. Bake at 150°C for 12 minutes until lightly coloured. While still hot, coat with vanilla sugar. Store in an airtight container.

Jam Strips

Preparation time:
  20 minutes
Cooking time:
  40 minutes
Makes about 24

1 1/4 cups plain flour,
  sifted
3/4 cup brown sugar
125 g butter
3/4 cup peach or apricot
  jam

1 Combine sifted flour and sugar in a bowl. Rub in butter with fingertips until the mixture resembles breadcrumbs. Press half of mixture over the base of a 20 cm square baking tin.
2 Spread jam carefully. Sprinkle over reserved half of flour mixture and press down lightly.
3 Bake at 180°C for 35-40 minutes, or until top is lightly browned. Cool in the tin then cut into strips to serve. Store in an airtight container.

Shortbread Caramel Slices

Preparation time:
  30 minutes
Cooking time:
  50 minutes
Makes about 16

Shortbread
1 cup plain flour, sifted
1/2 cup brown sugar
1/2 cup desiccated coconut
125 g butter, melted

Shortbread Caramel Slices

Caramel Filling
60 g butter
*2 tablespoons golden
  syrup*
400 g condensed milk

Chocolate Topping
*125 g cooking
  chocolate, chopped*
60 g butter

1 Combine sifted flour, sugar and coconut in a bowl. Mix in melted butter. Press into a greased 28 x 18 cm shallow oblong baking tin. Bake at 180°C for 25-30 minutes or until golden.
2 To make Filling: melt butter over low heat in a small pan. Stir in the golden syrup and condensed milk. Pour over cooked base and bake for 20 minutes. Set aside until cold.
3 To make Topping: melt chocolate and butter in a bowl over a pan of simmering water; stir to combine. Spread over cooled caramel filling. Mark in slices while setting. Refrigerate until set. Store in an airtight container.

HINT
The secret to crisp, tender and buttery shortbread lies with the kneading; gently knead the dough until it is very smooth.